JUSTIN LANGER COLOR

AUSTRALIAN CRICKETER

MR VIVEK KUMAR PANDEY SHAMBHUNATH

ISBN 979-888555667-5

Disclaimer : During Writing This Book No character & No religious , No Relation Members Are Harmed. It's Only For Study & Entertainment Purpose. Do Not Take Seriously. Short Biopic Written In This Book Written By Mr Vivek Kumar Pandey.

Contents

Foreword *vii*

Preface *ix*

1. Justin Langer Color 1

2. Australian Cricket history 9

3. Australia National Cricket Team 14

4. History Of Cricket 28

Foreword

Short biography of Justin langer and about life.During writing this book no character & no religious are harmed written by Mr Vivek Kumar Pandey. winner youngest writer award 1st rank in india 2020.He is only one writer can publish 790+ own book that was greatest successfull in his life.This All Credit Goes To My Super Hero Daddy. This book fully colour Edition.

Preface

Author biography in English :MY NAME IS VIVEK KUMAR PANDEY . I WAS BORN IN 30 SEP 2002,I AM FROM SURAT GUJARAT INDIA.MY DREAM WAS TO BE GOOD WRITERS ,MY FAMILY SUPPORTED ME TO SUCCESSFUL AND I CAN DO IT MY SELF.How do I write? That is a question, I believe, that can bc honestly answered by me."CELEBRATING YOUNGEST WRITER AWARD WINNER IN GUJARAT 1ST RANK" MR PANDEY JI . I may think I did a good job writing something . The reader is the one who decides the quality of my writing. I do find writing to be natural to me and therefore find it to be a real challenge. My trick as a challenged writer is to do the best I can and know that I am happy with the final outcome. It may take a while to do my best and there may be quite a few problems I run into along the way.

I am not a greedy person those who are thinking about me and my self I never tried it anyone people suffering from sadness ,I trying to get promoted people suffering from happiness and joy in your Life Time. Now in current situation in India and also world people are unemployed and have no many but our indian governor help to people to get free food from ration card , i also take part in leadership team ,i am Motivational speaker , Film script writer. There was my two dream firstly writer and secondly actor & also my own film is upcoming soon i done almost completely completed script for my film .I AM GOING TO SAY WORD OF HEART TOUCH OUT PLEASE READ IT" , firstly i thanks my father he supports me in this field they always getting inspired me by own his words and behavior ,they always said that he was a biggest person in the world in future and also they purchase fruit and chocolate for me in anytime & anyway , firstly my father buy him then call me Vivek you want a chocolate i will say yes papa but how many tell me ,papa: you tell me how much i buy him i told 1 or 2 chocolate but my father purchase whole the boxes of chocolate and they get suprised me. MY FATHER WAS BORN IN " 20 SEPTEMBER" 1971 IN INDIA.

1) MY FATHER FAVORITE CLOTHES IS KURTA PAIJMA AND ALSO STYLES SHOE

2) FAVORITE SINGER IS KISHORE DA

3) FAVORITE STATE GUJARAT AND KOLKATA , HIS VILLAGE IN BIHAR

4) FAVORITE COLOR BLACK AND WHITE

THEY ALSO LOVE cricket like IPL and one day t-20 .they also like watching a News daily and heard the song daily ,they also interested in tik tok video but in current time tik tok is banned in india but also few videos are in you tube. In lockdown time my family and me very enjoy day daily. my father play daily ludo with his sister and son, daughter.they always loved tea and coffee anytime call me "। विवेक थोड़ा चाय बनाओना विवेक तुम्हारे हाथ का चाय अच्छा लगता है". I make it tea for my father but some reason after the April to june they are suffering from fever and cough , weakness on 6 June 2020 my father death. they not told me say bye bye his life. After death of 6 June on 10 june my mom and dad anniversary.but my father is Best in the world they can do anything for me please take care of father and respect it of your parents.

CHAPTER ONE

Justin langer Color

- Justin Langer Color

1. Disclaimer : During Writing This Book No character & No religious , No Relation Members Are Harmed. It's Only For Study & Entertainment Purpose. Do Not Take Seriously. Short Biopic Written In This Book Written By Mr Vivek Kumar Pandey.

Justin Lee Langer AM (born 21 November 1970) is an Australian cricket coach and former cricketer. He is the current coach of the Australia men's national team, having been appointed to the role in May 2018. A left-handed batsman, Langer is best known for his partnership with Matthew Hayden as Australia's test opening batsmen during the early and mid-2000s, considered one of the most successful ever. Representing Western Australia domestically, Langer played English county cricket for Middlesex and also Somerset. He holds the record for the most runs scored at first-class level by an Australian.

Born in Perth, Western Australia, Langer excelled at cricket from an early age, representing Western Australia at under-age level, as well as the Australia under-19 team. He also won a scholarship to the Australian Cricket Academy at the Australian Institute of Sport in 1990. Langer made his first-class debut for Western Australia during the 1991–92 Sheffield Shield, and, after good form at state level, made his Test debut for Australia the following season at the age of 22, during the West Indies' 1992–93 tour.

Although maintaining his place in the side, he struggled for form, and only made sporadic appearances for Australia until his selection for Australia's 1998–99 tour of Pakistan, in which he scored his first Test century. Establishing himself at number three in the batting order, Langer maintained this role until the 2001 Ashes series. Having been injured for the first four Tests, he replaced Michael Slater as Matthew Hayden's opening partner for the final Test, and scored a century in Australia's innings win. This was the first of three centuries in consecutive matches that secured Langer's position at the top of the order.

Except for injuries, the partnership between Hayden and Langer (with Ricky Ponting moving to Langer's previous position at number three) persisted until Langer's retirement at the conclusion of the 2006–07 Ashes series. Their partnership included a total of 5,655 runs over a period of 113 innings, second only to the partnership between West Indians Gordon Greenidge and Desmond Haynes. Langer's retirement came after several injuries had restricted his batting, including a concussion sustained during Australia's 2005–06 tour of South Africa. Despite having been one of the leading runscorers in Australia's domestic limited-overs competition, he only played eight One Day International matches for Australia, all during a period from 1994 to 1997.

After his retirement, Langer played one final season with Western Australia (having served as the state's captain since the 2002–03 season), as well as continuing as captain of Somerset in English domestic cricket. He retired from all forms of the cricket at the end of the 2009 English cricket season. Langer was the Australian national cricket team's batting coach and senior assistant coach from November 2009 until November 2012, when he was appointed senior coach of the Perth Scorchers and Western Australia.

In 2016, Langer became interim coach for the Australian team while then coach Darren Lehmann took leave to scout for the Ashes and away matches late in 2016. In a fan poll conducted by the CA in 2017, he was named in the country's best Ashes XI in the last 40 years.

On 3 May 2018, Langer was announced as coach of the Australian national cricket team, following a ball tampering scandal which led to the resignation of Darren Lehmann. His four-year term began on 22 May 2018.

- Justin Langer 1993–2000

Langer made his Test debut against the West Indies at the Adelaide Oval, in January 1993. He received a rough welcome against an in-form West Indian bowling attack, and along with the rest of the Australian team, he took numerous blows from their pace bowlers.After only managing to score 20 in the first innings, Langer top-scored for Australia with 54 in the second, a famous chase by Australia that fell just 2 runs short. In the fifth and final Test of the series, Langer only managed to score 11 runs between his two innings in a match that was dominated by the bowling of Curtly Ambrose and Ian Bishop.

He retained his place for the following tour of New Zealand. After decent but not awe-inspiring totals in the first two Tests (63 & 24), Langer suffered the indignity of getting a pair in the third Test, falling for a duck in both innings. He was subsequently dropped, and other than a few scattered appearances did not return to the Australian Test team until October 1998, for the tour of Pakistan.

In November 1999 at Bellerive Oval in Hobart, he shared a match-winning 238-run partnership with Adam Gilchrist to rescue Australia from 126/5 chasing a victory target of 369 against Pakistan. The century scored in this innings was scored in 388 minutes, an Australian record for the slowest century.

- Justin Langer 2001–2002

Langer was a number three batsman until 2001 when he was dropped after failing to convert a series of starts during Australia's 2–1 loss in India. During the second Test in Kolkata, he bowled a single over when V. V. S. Laxman and Rahul Dravid defied the Australian attack for the entirety of the fourth day, forcing captain Steve Waugh to try almost all his players as bowlers; it was the only time Langer ever bowled at Test level.

Shortly after though, he replaced Michael Slater as an opening batsman for the final 2001 Ashes series Test at The Oval where he celebrated his return with a century. He did not get dropped again and as an opening batsman he averaged 52.38 and scored 14 centuries in 44 matches; previously he scored 7 centuries in 41 matches at an average of 39.04. Langer returned to Australia in the 2002–03 Ashes series, where his very successful partnership with Matthew Hayden developed. In this series, Langer scored his top score of 250 against England at the Melbourne Cricket Ground.

- Justin Langer 2003–2007

Langer personally outscored the entire Pakistan side in the Perth Test of 2004. He scored 191 and 97 while Pakistan made 179 and 72. It was the first occasion of a player being dismissed in both the 190s and 90s in a Test.

He captained the Prime Minister's XI in December 2005 in their match against the West Indies.

In the 2005 Ashes series, Langer top-scored for an unsuccessful Australian team, with 391 in the series. His top score was 105, scored in the final test.

After this, pressure was mounting on the opening partnership of Hayden and Langer. Calls were coming to have the pair replaced by a younger duo, that would ensure the future and stability of the team to come. However, the partnership had support from the Australian selectors and was only disrupted in the 2006 Summer series when Langer was out with injury. He was replaced by Mike Hussey and Phil Jaques for two tests.

Langer then suffered a number of injuries, increasing the pressure on selectors to drop him for rising star Phil Jaques. Langer was selected over Jaques for the 2007 Ashes series, which turned out to be his last. Langer scored an 80 and a century in the first test, but it was slim pickings to follow for him.

Despite success in the Australian Test team, he did not get recalled to the one-day team, even after he was named as the domestic ING Cup's player of the season in 2002/03.

- Justin Langer Retirement

On 1 January 2007, Langer announced his retirement from Test cricket after the fifth Ashes Test against England, starting at the Sydney Cricket Ground the following day. In doing so, he joined Shane Warne and Glenn McGrath who had both announced their retirements earlier in the month, and it came only three matches after the surprise departure of Damien Martyn. He came to the decision during the previous match in Melbourne, having earlier decided against retiring after the tour of South Africa to help Australia reclaim the Ashes. He said of his decision: "Everyone keeps saying 'you'll know when it's time'. Well, at one o'clock two days ago I knew it was time – it just came to me."

Despite his retirement from international cricket, Langer opted to continue to play first-class cricket, with Somerset announcing on the same day that Langer had agreed to return to the English county in 2007 as captain. Langer had said during his retirement announcement that he was relishing returning to Somerset: "There's an amazing challenge at Somerset.

They're at the bottom of everything, and I've got a great regard for the coach over there and I'm looking forward to that challenge." Langer also stayed on with Western Australia for a final season in 2007–08.

- Justin Langer Centuries

Langer made 23 centuries in international cricket, all in Tests. As of March 2019 he sits joint fifty-sixth in the list of century-makers in international cricket.

He scored his first Test century against Pakistan at the Arbab Niaz Stadium, Peshawar on 15 October 1998, scoring 116. He scored his final Test century against England at The Gabba, Brisbane on 23 November 2006 and his final Test match was the final game of the same series at the Sydney Cricket Ground, Sydney on 2 January 2007, having played 105 matches. His highest score in Tests is 250, scored against England at the Melbourne Cricket Ground, Melbourne on 26 December 2002.

He never made a century in the ODI format; his highest score was 36, which he made against India at the Sharjah Cricket Stadium, Sharjah on 19 April 1994.

- Justin Langer Domestic career

Langer was the captain of the Western Warriors until the end of the 2006/2007 season. He became the highest run-scorer for Western Australia in 4-day matches, after passing Tom Moody's old record of 8853 runs on 5 December 2007 against Tasmania at Bellerive Oval. On 5 March 2008, Langer announced his retirement from Australian first-class domestic cricket. Earlier in the year, Langer had announced his retirement from the Australian domestic one-day cricket. However, Langer said that he would play another season for Somerset in county cricket. Langer played for Western Australia in a career spanning 17 years, leaving as the highest run-scorer in Western Australia's history.

- Justin Langer (County Cricket)

Langer played county cricket for Middlesex County Cricket Club from 1998 to 2000, captaining the side in 2000. In his first season, he scored his maiden century in English domestic cricket in superb fashion with 233 not out against Somerset at Lord's, in the same match that he was awarded his county cap. He went on to score centuries in his next two County Championship matches, and achieved 1,000 runs for the season after only eight matches. He finished the season with the second highest runs total and batting average in the Championship, behind John Crawley on both counts.

- Langer as captain at Somerset, 27 June 2007

In June 2006 it was announced that he would join Somerset later that month for six weeks, while fellow countryman Dan Cullen was on duty with Australia A. On 20 July 2006, he made his highest first-class score of 342 playing for Somerset in a County Championship match against Surrey at the Woodbridge Road ground in Guildford. This was also the highest score ever by a Somerset batsman, breaking the record of Sir Viv Richards who made 322 against Warwickshire at Taunton in 1985, and is the 10th highest score in a first-class match in England. During his six-week spell at the club, Langer also enjoyed particular success in the Twenty20 competition, topping the batting charts along with fellow Australian Cameron White.

On 20 April 2007 he became the first Somerset player to score two triple centuries in the County Championship when he hit 315 against Middlesex in a match noted for its batting. Responding to a Middlesex first innings of 600, Somerset set a new ground record at the County Ground, Taunton with 850–7 declared. On 19 September 2007 it was announced that Langer would stay with Somerset (as captain) for the 2008 season. In 15 first-class matches for the county in 2007, Langer scored 1215 runs at 57.85 and a further 764 in one-day competitions.

Early in the 2008 season, Langer and Marcus Trescothick put on a 272-second wicket partnership during the second innings against Hampshire at the County Ground, Taunton; falling just 18 short of the 1924 ground record.

On 23 July 2009, playing his 615th innings, he surpassed Sir Donald Bradman as the leading Australian first-class run scorer when he scored his 86th century whilst playing Worcestershire. At the end of the 2009 season, Langer announced that he would not be returning to Taunton in a playing capacity the following season, and retiring from all competitive cricket. He commented in an interview with BBC Somerset that he was in discussions to potentially return at some point to the county in the future in a coaching capacity.

Langer played his last home game in English domestic cricket on 27 September 2009, captaining Somerset against Durham in the Nat West Pro40. A game which Somerset lost by two runs. Langer's last act as Somerset captain was to lead the side to the second stage of the 2009 Twenty20 Champions League.

- Justin Langer Post-playing career

Langer through to the end of his career remained publicly undecided about what he wanted to do after his retirement. Speculation hence rose in the media with suggestions of a coaching position with Middlesex, and an open invitation to return to Somerset in some capacity. In November 2009, Cricket Australia announced the appointment of Langer as assistant coach of their Test team under national boss Tim Nielsen, as a batting coach and mentor. In November 2012, Langer was appointed to the position of senior coach of Western Australia and the Perth Scorchers, after the resignation of Lachlan Stevens, with a contract until the end of the 2015–16 season.In July 2017, Langer was appointed to the board of the West Coast Eagles football club.

In May 2018, Langer was announced as the coach of the Australian national cricket team, and then in October 2019, Andrew McDonald was appointed as his assistant coach. In 2019, he coached Australia to the semi-finals of the 2019 Cricket World Cup, losing to England by 8 wickets. It was noted before the game that Langer had got Australia to walk barefoot around the edge of Edgbaston before the match in a bid to capture "positive energy coming out of the earth".

- Justin Langer Famous duels and partner

In his 100th test, Langer was hit by a bouncer from Makhaya Ntini (South Africa v Australia, 3rd Test, Johannesburg, 2nd day). He suffered concussion and underwent scans in hospital. Despite the risk of being killed if hit on the head again, Langer padded up to bat in the second innings if it was required of him. Captain Ricky Ponting wrote in his diary that because of Langer's intention of defying medical advice, he would have had to declare the run chase and forfeit the match to prevent Langer from facing the bowling. Brett Lee scored the winning runs before Langer was needed.

Langer's most notable opening batting partner was Matthew Hayden. The opening pair represented Australia in more than 100 Test innings. The pair made 5654 runs while batting together in partnerships, with an average of 51 runs per partnership; only Gordon Greenidge and Desmond Haynes of the West Indies have scored more Test runs as a partnership, with 6482.

- Justin Langer Personal life

Langer is an old boy of Perth schools Newman College and Aquinas College.The Justin Langer Shield is played between year sevens of Newman and Aquinas.

He is the nephew of Rob Langer, a left-handed batsman for Western Australia during the 1970s and 1980s. Langer is married to his high school sweetheart, Sue, and has four daughters. When resident in Somerset, the family stayed in a rented home in Hatch Beauchamp: "Mate, I say this with the utmost affection and respect, but it's like living in the olden days."He is a martial artist and has obtained the rank of Shodan-Ho (probationary 1st degree black belt) in Zen Do Kai.

Langer has written five books. His first was entitled From Outback to Outfield: A Revealing Diary of Life on the County Cricket Circuit. His second, an autobiography released after his return from rock bottom in 2001, entitled The Power of Passion. He also released a book with Steve Harmison entitled Ashes Frontline: The Ashes War Diaries of Steve Harmison and Justin Langer about the 2006–07 Ashes series in Australia. He also wrote Seeing the Sunrise which has been described as "a handbook for overcoming self-doubt, for revelling in success, for aiming high. It is about mastering physical and mental goals, enjoying victories and fighting adversity." His most recent book is Keeping My Head: A Life in Cricket.

Melbourne rock band Telemachus Brown wrote a song about Langer entitled (Wrong about) Justin Langer. It was released on their 2006 EP Medicine Songs and was a hit for the band on Melbourne university radio. The song could be a reference to Langer's transformation from being an average Test batsman in his early career to a world-class opener later in his career.

Langer is a devout Catholic, as was his Australian opening batsman partner Matthew Hayden. Politically, he is conservative, an admirer of former Liberal Australian Prime Minister John Howard, and considered running for office as a member of the Liberal Party of Australia.

CHAPTER TWO

Australian Cricket history

- Australian Cricket history

Australian Cricket has a history spanning over 200 years. The earliest reports of the sport in Australia appeared in the Sydney Gazette - the first newspaper printed in the country in 1804 - and by 1826 there were records of clubs being formed in Sydney.

By 1832, clubs were forming in Tasmania; known at the time as Van Diemen's Land. In Western Australia, there is a record of labourers and mechanics taking on the builders of the new Government House as far back as 1835. The Melbourne Cricket Club was formed in 1838, and South Australia was participating in club cricket by 1839. From east to west, the sport was beginning to animate all corners of the nation.

In 1851, Victorians travelled to Tasmania to play the first intercolonial match, with 15,000 spectators in attendance. Such matches were known as Intercolonial matches until Federation in 1901, when they became Interstate matches.

1. The burgeoning sport required administration, with Boards of Control formed in New South Wales in 1857, Victoria in 1864 and South Australia in 1871.
2. There were tours of Australia by English sides in the summers of 1861/62 and 1863/64 before a team of Indigenous Australians became the first side to make a reciprocal tour to the northern hemisphere in the summer of 1868. That tour was led by Charles Lawrence, an Englishman who was part of the 1861/62 tour to Australia. He liked the country so much, he decided to stay.

3. Another English side – including the most famous player of the era, Dr W G Grace – toured Australia in 1873/74 before, in 1876/77, a combined New South Wales and Victorian side took on a touring English team at the Melbourne Cricket Ground for what became recognised as the first Test match. The Australians won by 45 runs and the match included an innings of 165 "not out" by the home side's Charles Bannerman, the first individual three-figure score in Test history.
4. An Australian side toured England in 1878 but the first Test match there did not occur until 1880 when the two sides met at The Oval in London. In 1882, after Australia's first victory on English soil, the legend of The Ashes – the mythical trophy that the two countries compete for in Test match cricket – began.
5. The Sheffield Shield domestic competition in Australia was initiated in 1892 by the Australasian Cricket Council, the first attempt at a national governing body. The Shield was the result of a donation by Lord Sheffield, the financier of an England tour of Australia in 1891/92.

As for the Council, it featured representatives of New South Wales, Victoria and South Australia with the aim of regulating Intercolonial cricket and organising international tours.

That latter role was one the players resisted, as private tours were a means for them to earn a living by playing the game. Indeed, in 1912, six of Australia's leading players - Warwick Armstrong, Vernon Ransford, Victor Trumper, Tibby Cotter, Hanson Carter and Clem Hill - all declined to tour England for a triangular tournament that also involved South Africa.

The public motive for their disquiet was that their choice of team manager had been rejected by the Australian Board of Control for International Cricket – the body formed in 1905 to replace the Australasian Cricket Council, which had been disbanded in 1899. But the underlying reason was the question of who should have access to the funds raised by such tours.

The trip took place without what became known as "The Big Six" and the control of the game by administrators over players became established. Armstrong would later go on to captain Australia to its first-ever clean-sweep of an Ashes series, a 5-0 success against a war-ravaged England team in 1920/21. That victory was spearheaded by fast bowlers Jack Gregory and Ted McDonald, establishing another principle in cricket that was to stand the test of time – whichever side had the best pace bowlers was more likely to prevail.

- The Meeting

The first meeting of the Australian Board of Control for International Cricket featured two representatives from each of New South Wales and Victoria. For its second meeting one delegate from Queensland was permitted to attend, and in 1906, three representatives of New South Wales, South Australia and Victoria plus one Queenslander were present. Tasmania's first delegate attended in 1907 and six years later they were joined by a single Western Australia official.

In 1914 and 1974 respectively, Queensland and Western Australia increased their representation to two delegates. By 1973, the body had become the Australian Cricket Board. It stayed that way until 2003, when the game's national governing body became Cricket Australia.

- The Sheffield Shield

The Sheffield Shield was played between three states – New South Wales, South Australia and Victoria – from its inception in 1892 until 1926/27, when Queensland joined. Western Australia was admitted in 1947/48 and Tasmania became the sixth state to play in the competition in 1977/78. Matches were timeless up to 1926/27, before becoming four-day contests. From 1982/83 the top two sides in the competition each season have played off in a final.

The first domestic one-day competition took place in the summer of 1969/70, although New Zealand competed until 1974/75, claiming victory three times. The Australian Capital Territory (ACT) had a side compete for three seasons from 1997/98.

- domestic Twenty20 tournament

A domestic Twenty20 tournament started in 2005/06. For its first six seasons, the competition was state-based before it was replaced by the Big Bash League in 2011/12 featuring eight teams; two each from New South Wales and Victoria plus one from Adelaide, Perth, Brisbane and Hobart. Unlike several other Twenty20 competitions around the world, Cricket Australia - as the governing body - retained overall control of the teams.

- Women Cricket After Progress

The history of women in cricket can be traced back to 1894, when a Tasmanian created the first local women's competition in Australia's history books. In 1931, the Australian Women's Cricket Association would form, with the Australian women's team taking to the world stage against England in 1934 in the first ever Test match. From Ruby Monaghan to Ellyse Perry. From grassroots to elite. This is the evolution of women's cricket in Australia.

Women's cricket in Australia is believed to have started in 1894 when a Tasmanian, Lily Poulett-Harris, created a local competition. Just over a decade later, in 1905, the Victorian Women's Cricket Association was formed, followed by the Australian Women's Cricket Association in 1931.

During the summer of 1930/31, the first Australian Women's National Cricket Championships (WNCC) took place. Three years, later women's international cricket was born when the Australian Women's Cricket Council invited the Women's Cricket Association of England to send a team on tour. That trip featured 14 three-day matches and included the first-ever Women's Test match.

From 1972/73, Australian domestic teams have taken part in the WNCC and play for the Ruth Preddey Cup, named after the former New South Wales player and journalist who helped to organize finance for a tour of England herself. A women's Twenty20 Cup was first played at national level in 2008/09, although the Australian Capital Territory and Tasmania were not admitted until the following summer.

The governing body for the women's game then merged with Cricket Australia in 2003, ensuring that the men's and women's sport was run by one single and unified body. That body formed the Women's Big Bash League; a domestic Twenty20 competition featuring the same sides as the men's short-form tournament in 2015.

- Today Women Cricket

In 2018, a record breaking 1,558,821 Australians actively engaged in cricket competitions or programs across the nation; an increase on nine per cent from the previous year. Six in every 10 new participants were females, and multicultural participation rose by four per cent, making up 22 per cent of all participants. Indigenous participation is also on the rise, with an increased participation level of one per cent.

CHAPTER THREE

Australia National Cricket Team

- Australia National Cricket Team

The Australia men's national cricket team represents Australia in men's international cricket. As the joint oldest team in Test cricket history, playing in the first ever Test match in 1877, the team also plays One-Day International (ODI) and Twenty20 International (T20I) cricket, participating in both the first ODI, against England in the 1970–71 season and the first T20I, against New Zealand in the 2004–05 season, winning both games. The team draws its players from teams playing in the Australian domestic competitions – the Sheffield Shield, the Australian domestic limited-overs cricket tournament and the Big Bash League.

The national team has played 837 Test matches, winning 397, losing 226, drawing 212 and tying 2. As of January 2021, Australia is ranked third in the ICC Test Championship on 113 rating points. Australia is the most successful team in Test cricket history, in terms of overall wins, win-loss ratio and wins percentage.

Test rivalries include The Ashes (with England), The Border-Gavaskar Trophy (with India), the Frank Worrell Trophy (with the West Indies), the Trans-Tasman Trophy (with New Zealand), and with South Africa.

The team has played 958 ODI matches, winning 581, losing 334, tying 9 and with 34 ending in a no-result. As of January 2021, Australia is ranked fourth in the ICC ODI Championship on 111 rating points, though have been ranked first for 141 of 185 months since its introduction in 2002.

Australia is the most successful team in ODI cricket history, winning more than 60 per cent of their matches, with a record seven World Cup final appearances (1975, 1987, 1996, 1999, 2003, 2007 and 2015) and have won the World Cup a record five times: 1987, 1999, 2003, 2007 and 2015. Australia is the first (and only) team to appear in four consecutive World Cup finals (1996, 1999, 2003 and 2007), surpassing the old record of three consecutive World Cup appearances by the West Indies (1975, 1979 and 1983) and the first and only team to win 3 consecutive World Cups (1999, 2003 and 2007). The team was undefeated in 34 consecutive World Cup matches until the 2011 Cricket World Cup where Pakistan beat them by 4 wickets in the Group stage.

It is also the second team to win a World Cup (2015) on home soil, after India (2011). Australia have also won the ICC Champions Trophy twice (2006 and 2009) making them the first and the only team to become back to back winners in the Champions Trophy tournaments. As of 2021, Australia is the only team to win five Cricket World Cups; no other team has won more than two.

The national team has played 153 Twenty20 International matches, winning 79, losing 69, tying 2 and with 3 ending in a no-result. As of November 2021, Australia is ranked sixth in the ICC T20I Championship on 246 rating points. Australia are the reigning ICC Men's T20 World Cup champions, defeating New Zealand in the 2021 final to claim their first T20 World Cup title.

On 12 January 2019, Australia won the first ODI against India at the Sydney Cricket Ground by 34 runs, to record their 1,000th win in international cricket.

- Australian cricket from 1876–77 to 1890

The Australian team that toured England in 1878

The Australian cricket team participated in the first Test match at the MCG in 1877, defeating an English team by 45 runs, with Charles Bannerman making the first Test century, a score of 165 retired hurt.Test cricket, which only occurred between Australia and England at the time, was limited by the long distance between the two countries, which would take several months by sea. Despite Australia's much smaller population, the team was very competitive in early games, producing stars such as Jack Blackham, Billy Murdoch, Fred "The Demon" Spofforth, George Bonnor, Percy McDonnell, George Giffen and Charles "The Terror" Turner. Most cricketers at the time were either from New South Wales or Victoria, with the notable exception of George Giffen, the star South Australian all-rounder.

A highlight of Australia's early history was the 1882 Test match against England at The Oval. In this match, Fred Spofforth took 7/44 in the game's fourth innings to save the match by preventing England from making their 85-run target. After this match The Sporting Times, a major newspaper in London at the time, printed a mock obituary in which the death of English cricket was proclaimed and the announcement made that "the body was cremated and the ashes taken to Australia." This was the start of the famous Ashes series in which Australia and England play a series of Test matches to decide the holder of the Ashes. To this day, the contest is one of the fiercest rivalries in sport.

- Golden age

History of Australian cricket from 1890–91 to 1900 and History of Australian cricket from 1900–01 to 1918

The so-called 'Golden Age' of Australian Test cricket occurred around the end of the 19th century and the beginning of the 20th century, with the team under the captaincy of Joe Darling, Monty Noble and Clem Hill winning eight of ten tours. It is considered to have lasted from the 1897–98 English tour of Australia and the 1910–11 South African tour of Australia. Outstanding batsmen such as Joe Darling, Clem Hill, Reggie Duff, Syd Gregory, Warren Bardsley and Victor Trumper, brilliant all-rounders including Monty Noble, George Giffen, Harry Trott and Warwick Armstrong and excellent bowlers including Ernie Jones, Hugh Trumble, Tibby Cotter, Bill Howell, Jack Saunders and Bill Whitty, all helped Australia to become the dominant cricketing nation for most of this period.

Victor Trumper became one of Australia's first sporting heroes, and was widely considered Australia's greatest batsman before Bradman and one of the most popular players. He played a record (at the time) number of Tests at 49 and scored 3163 (another record) runs at a high for the time average of 39.04. His early death in 1915 at the age of 37 from kidney disease caused national mourning. The Wisden Cricketers' Almanack, in its obituary for him, called him Australia's greatest batsman: "Of all the great Australian batsmen Victor Trumper was by general consent the best and most brilliant."

The years leading up to the start of World War I were marred by conflict between the players, led by Clem Hill, Victor Trumper and Frank Laver, the Australian Board of Control for International Cricket, led by Peter McAlister, who was attempting to gain more control of tours from the players. This led to six leading players (the so-called "Big Six") walking out on the 1912 Triangular Tournament in England, with Australia fielding what was generally considered a second-rate side. This was the last series before the war, and no more cricket was played by Australia for eight years, with Tibby Cotter being killed in Palestine during the war.

- Australian cricket from 1918–19 to 1930

Test cricket resumed in the 1920/21 season in Australia with a touring English team, captained by Johnny Douglas losing all five Tests to Australia, captained by the "Big Ship" Warwick Armstrong. Several players from before the war, including Warwick Armstrong, Charlie Macartney, Charles Kelleway, Warren Bardsley and the wicket-keeper Sammy Carter, were instrumental in the team's success, as well as new players Herbie Collins, Jack Ryder, Bert Oldfield, the spinner Arthur Mailey and the so-called "twin destroyers" Jack Gregory and Ted McDonald. The team continued its success on the 1921 tour of England, winning three out of the five Tests in Warwick Armstrong's last series. The side was, on the whole, inconsistent in the latter half of the 1920s, losing its first home Ashes series since the 1911–12 season in 1928–29.

- Australian cricket from 1930–31 to 1945

The 1930 tour of England heralded a new age of success for the Australian team. The team, led by Bill Woodfull – the "Great Un-bowlable" – featured legends of the game including Bill Ponsford, Stan McCabe, Clarrie Grimmett and the young pair of Archie Jackson and Don Bradman. Bradman was the outstanding batsman of the series, scoring a record 974 runs, including one century, two double centuries and one triple century, a massive score of 334 at Leeds which including 309 runs in a day. Jackson died of tuberculosis at the age of 23 three years later, after playing eight Tests. The team was widely considered unstoppable, winning nine of its next ten Tests.

The 1932–33 England tour of Australia is considered one of the most infamous episodes of cricket, due to the England team's use of bodyline, where captain Douglas Jardine instructed his bowlers Bill Voce and Harold Larwood to bowl fast, short-pitched deliveries aimed at the bodies of the Australian batsmen. The tactic, although effective, was widely considered by Australian crowds as vicious and unsporting. Injuries to Bill Woodfull, who was struck over the heart, and Bert Oldfield, who received a fractured skull (although from a non-bodyline ball), exacerbated the situation, almost causing a full-scale riot from the 50 000 fans at the Adelaide Oval for the third Test.

The conflict almost escalated into a diplomatic incident between the two countries, as leading Australian political figures, including the Governor of South Australia, Alexander Hore-Ruthven, protested to their English counterparts. The series ended in a 4–1 win for England but the bodyline tactics used were banned the year after.

The Australian team put the result of this series behind them, winning their next tour of England in 1934. The team was led by Bill Woodfull on his final tour and was notably dominated by Ponsford and Bradman, who twice put on partnerships of over 380 runs, with Bradman once again scoring a triple-century at Leeds. The bowling was dominated by the spin pair of Bill O'Reilly and Clarrie Grimmett, who took 53 wickets between them, with O'Reilly twice taking seven-wicket hauls.

Sir Donald Bradman is widely considered the greatest batsman of all time. He dominated the sport from 1930 until his retirement in 1948, setting new records for the highest score in a Test innings (334 vs England at Headingley in 1930), the most runs (6996), the most centuries (29), the most double centuries and the highest Test and first-class batting averages. His record for the highest Test batting average – 99.94 – has never been beaten. It is almost 40 runs per innings above the next highest average. He would have finished with an average of over 100 runs per innings if he had not been dismissed for a duck in his last Test. He was knighted in 1949 for services to cricket. He is generally considered one of Australia's greatest sporting heroes.

Test cricket was again interrupted by war, with the last Test series in 1938 made notable by Len Hutton scoring a world record 364 for England, with Chuck Fleetwood-Smith conceding 298 runs in England's world record total of 7/903. Ross Gregory, a notable young batsman who played two Tests before the war, was killed in the war.

- Australian cricket from 1945–46 to 1960

The team continued its success after the end of the Second World War, with the first Test (also Australia's first against New Zealand) being played in the 1945–46 season against New Zealand. Australia was by far the most successful team of the 1940s, being undefeated throughout the decade, winning two Ashes series against England and its first Test series against India. The team capitalised on its ageing stars Bradman, Sid Barnes, Bill Brown and Lindsay Hassett while new talent, including Ian Johnson, Don Tallon, Arthur Morris, Neil Harvey, Bill Johnston and the fast bowling pair of Ray Lindwall and Keith Miller, who all made their debut in the latter half of the 1940s, and were to form the basis of the team for a good part of the next decade. The team that Don Bradman led to England in 1948 gained the moniker The Invincibles, after going through the tour without losing a single game.

Of 31 first-class games played during the tour, they won 23 and drew 8, including winning the five-match Test series 4–0, with one draw. The tour was particularly notable for the fourth Test of the series, in which Australia won by seven wickets chasing a target of 404, setting a new record for the highest run chase in Test cricket, with Arthur Morris and Bradman both scoring centuries, as well as for the final Test in the series, Bradman's last, where he finished with a duck in his last innings after needing only four runs to secure a career average of 100.

Australia was less successful in the 1950s, losing three consecutive Ashes series to England, including a horrendous 1956 Tour of England, where the 'spin twins' Laker and Lock destroyed Australia, taking 61 wickets between them, including Laker taking 19 wickets in the game (a first-class record) at Headingley, a game dubbed Laker's Match.

However, the team rebounded to win five consecutive series in the latter half of the 1950s, first under the leadership of Ian Johnson, then Ian Craig and Richie Benaud. The series against the West Indies in the 1960–61 season was notable for the Tied Test in the first game at the Gabba, which was the first in Test cricket. Australia ended up winning the series 2–1 after a hard-fought series that was praised for its excellent standards and sense of fair play. Stand-out players in that series as well as through the early part of the 1960s were Richie Benaud, who took a then-record number of wickets as a leg-spinner and who also captained Australia in 28 Tests, including 24 without defeat; Alan Davidson, who was a notable fast-bowler and also became the first player to take 10 wickets and make 100 runs in the same game in the first Test; Bob Simpson, who also later captained Australia for two different periods of time; Colin McDonald, the first-choice opening batsman for most of the 1950s and early '60s; Norm O'Neill, who made 181 in the Tied Test; Neil Harvey, towards the end of his long career; and Wally Grout, an excellent wicket-keeper who died at the age of 41.

- World Series Cricket and Restructuring

The Centenary Test was played in March 1977 at the MCG to celebrate 100 years since the first Test was played. Australia won the match by 45 runs, an identical result to the first Test match.

In May 1977, Kerry Packer announced he was organising a breakaway competition – World Series Cricket (WSC) – after the Australian Cricket Board (ACB) refused to accept Channel Nine's bid to gain exclusive television rights to Australia's Test matches in 1976. Packer secretly signed leading international cricketers to his competition, including 28 Australians. Almost all of the Australian Test team at the time were signed to WSC – notable exceptions including Gary Cosier, Geoff Dymock, Kim Hughes and Craig Serjeant – and the Australian selectors were forced to pick what was generally considered a third-rate team from players in the Sheffield Shield. Former player Bob Simpson, who had retired 10 years previously after a conflict with the board, was recalled at the age of 41 to captain Australia against India. Jeff Thomson was named deputy in a team that included seven debutants. Australia managed to win the series 3–2, mainly thanks to the batting of Simpson, who scored 539 runs, including two centuries; and the bowling of Wayne Clark, who took 28 wickets.

Australia lost the next series 3–1 against the West Indies, which was fielding a full strength team; and also lost the 1978–79 Ashes series 5–1, the team's worst Ashes result in Australia. Graham Yallop was named as captain for the Ashes, with Kim Hughes taking over for the 1979–80 tour of India. Rodney Hogg took 41 wickets in his debut series, an Australian record. WSC players returned to the team for the 1979–80 season after a settlement between the ACB and Kerry Packer. Greg Chappell was reinstated as captain.

The underarm bowling incident of 1981 occurred when, in an ODI against New Zealand, Greg Chappell instructed his brother Trevor to bowl an underarm delivery to New Zealand batsman Brian McKechnie, with New

Zealand needing a six to tie off the last ball. The aftermath of the incident soured political relations between Australia and New Zealand, with several leading political and cricketing figures calling it "unsportsmanlike" and "not in the spirit of cricket".

Australia continued its success up until the early 1980s, built around the Chappell brothers, Dennis Lillee, Jeff Thomson and Rod Marsh. The 1980s was a period of relative mediocrity after the turmoil caused by the Rebel Tours of South Africa and the subsequent retirement of several key players. The rebel tours were funded by the South African Cricket Board to compete against its national side, which had been banned—along with many other sports, including Olympic athletes—from competing internationally, due to the South African government's racist apartheid policies. Some of Australia's best players were poached: Graham Yallop, Carl Rackemann, Terry Alderman, Rodney Hogg, Kim Hughes, John Dyson, Greg Shipperd, Steve Rixon and Steve Smith amongst others. These players were handed three-year suspensions by the Australian Cricket Board which greatly weakened the player pool for the national sides, as most were either current representative players or on the verge of gaining honours.

- Australian cricket from 1985–86 to 2000

The so-called 'Golden Era' of Australian cricket occurred around the end of the 20th century and the beginning of the 21st century. This was a period in which Australian cricket recovered from the disruption caused by World Series Cricket to create arguably the strongest Test team in history.

Under the captaincy of Allan Border and the new fielding standards put in place by new coach Bob Simpson, the team was restructured and gradually rebuilt their cricketing stocks. Some of the rebel players returned to the national side after serving their suspensions, including Trevor Hohns, Carl Rackemann and Terry Alderman. During these lean years, it was the batsmen Border, David Boon, Dean Jones, the young Steve Waugh and the bowling feats of Alderman, Bruce Reid, Craig McDermott, Merv Hughes and to a lesser extent, Geoff Lawson who kept the Australian side afloat.

With the emergence of players such as Ian Healy, Mark Taylor, Geoff Marsh, Mark Waugh, and Greg Matthews in the late 1980s, Australia was on the way back from the doldrums. Winning the Ashes in 1989, the Australians got a roll on beating Pakistan, Sri Lanka and then followed it up with another Ashes win on home soil in 1991. The Australians went on to the West Indies and had their chances but ended up losing the series. However, they bounced back and beat the Indians in their next Test series. With the retirement of the champion but defensive, Allan Border, a new era of attacking cricket had begun under the leadership of firstly Mark Taylor and then Steve Waugh.

The 1990s and early 21st century were arguably Australia's most successful periods, unbeaten in all Ashes series played bar the famous 2005 series and achieving a hat-trick of World Cups. This success has been attributed to the restructuring of the team and system by Border, successive aggressive captains, and the effectiveness of several key players, most notably Glenn McGrath, Shane Warne, Justin Langer, Matthew Hayden, Steve Waugh, Adam Gilchrist, Michael Hussey and Ricky Ponting.

- Australian cricket from 2000–01

Following the 2006–07 Ashes series which Australia won 5 nil, Australia slipped in the rankings after the retirements of key players. In the 2013/14 Ashes series, Australia again defeated England 5 nil and climbed back to third in the ICC International Test rankings. In February/March 2014, Australia beat South Africa, the number 1 team in the world, 2–1 and overtook them to return to the top of the rankings. In 2015, Australia won the World Cup, losing just one game for the tournament.

As of December 2020, Australia are ranked first in the ICC Test Championship, fourth in the ICC ODI Championship and second in the ICC T20I Championship.

- 2018 Australian ball-tampering scandal

On 25 March 2018, during the third Test match against hosts South Africa; players Cameron Bancroft, Steve Smith, David Warner and the leadership group of the team were implicated in a ball tampering scandal. Smith and Bancroft admitted to conspiring to alter the condition of the ball by rubbing it with a piece of adhesive tape containing abrasive granules picked up from the ground (it was later revealed that sandpaper was used). Smith stated that the purpose was to gain an advantage by unlawfully changing the ball's surface in order to generate reverse swing.

Bancroft had been filmed tampering with the ball and after being informed he had been caught, he was seen to transfer a yellow object from a pocket to the inside front of his trousers to hide the evidence. Steve Smith and David Warner were stood down as captain and vice-captain during the third Test while head coach, Darren Lehmann was suspected to have assisted Cameron Bancroft to tamper the ball.

The ICC imposed a one-match ban and 100%-match-fee fine on Smith, while Bancroft was fined 75 per cent of his match fee and received 3 demerit points. Smith and Warner were both stripped of their captaincy roles by Cricket Australia and sent home from the tour (along with Bancroft). Tim Paine was appointed as captain for the fourth Test. Cricket Australia then suspended Smith and Warner from playing for 12 months and Bancroft for 9 months. Smith and Bancroft could not be considered for leadership roles for 12 months after the suspension, while Warner is banned from leadership of any Cricket Australia team for life.

In the aftermath of these events, Darren Lehmann announced his resignation as head coach at the end of the series with Justin Langer replacing him. On 8 May 2018, Tim Paine was also named as the ODI captain while Aaron Finch was reinstated as T20I captain hours later, although Finch replaced Paine as the ODI captain after the 5-0 ODI series whitewash in England in June 2018.

On 7 October 2018, Australia played their first Test match under new coach Justin Langer and a new leadership group, which included Tim Paine as Australia's 46th Test captain. After a 1–0 loss to Pakistan in a two match Test series against Pakistan in the UAE and a 2–1 defeat against India in a four match Test series, they found success against Sri Lanka, winning the two Test match series 2–0.

In 2019, Australia played in the Cricket World Cup, where they finished second in the group stage before being knocked out by England at Edgbaston in the semi-final. Australia went on to retain the Ashes during the 2019 Ashes series, the first time on English soil since 2001, by winning the fourth Test at Old Trafford.

In 2020–21, Australia hosted India for 3 ODIs, 3 T20Is, and 4 Tests. They won the ODI series 2–1, but lost the T20I series 2–1. Then, the two teams competed for the Border-Gavaskar Trophy which saw one of the greatest overseas Test triumphs by India in the 4th Test to win the series 2–1 with the 3rd Test being drawn.

- Team colours

For Test matches, the team wears Cricket Whites, with an optional sweater or sweater-vest with a green and gold V-neck for use in cold weather. The sponsor's (currently Alinta for home matches and Qantas for away matches) logo is displayed on the right side of the chest while the Cricket Australia emblem is displayed on the left. If the sweater is being worn the Cricket Australia emblem is displayed under the V-neck and the sponsor's logo is again displayed on the right side of the chest. The baggy green, the Australian Test cricket cap, is considered an essential part of the cricketing uniform and as a symbol of the national team, with new players being presented with one upon their selection in the team. The cap and the helmet both prominently display the Australian cricketing coat-of-arms instead of the Cricket Australia emblem. At the end of 2011, ASICS was named the manufacturer of the whites and limited over uniforms from Adidas, with the ASICS logo being displayed on the shirt and pants. Players may choose any manufacturer for their other gear (bat, pads, shoes, gloves, etc.).

In One Day International (ODI) cricket and Twenty20 International cricket, the team wears uniforms usually coloured green and gold, the national colours of Australia. There has been a variety of different styles and layouts used in both forms of the limited-overs game, with coloured clothing (sometimes known as "pyjamas") being introduced for World Series Cricket in the late 1970s. The Alinta or Qantas logo is prominently displayed on the shirts and other gears. The current home ODI kit consists of green as the primary colour and gold as the secondary colour. The away kit is the opposite of the home kit with gold as the primary colour and green as the secondary colour. The home Twenty20 kit consists of black with the natural colours of Australia, green and gold strips. However, since Australia beat New Zealand at the MCG in the 2015 Cricket World Cup wearing the gold uniform, it has also become their primary colour, with the hats used being called 'floppy gold', formerly known as 'baggy gold', a limited-overs equivalent to a baggy green. Until the early 2000s and briefly in early 2020, in ODIs, Australia wore yellow helmets, before using green helmets as in test matches.

Former suppliers were Asics (1999), ISC (2000–2001), Fila (2002–2003) and Adidas (2004–2010) among others. Before Travelex, some of the former sponsors were Coca-Cola (1993–1998), Fly Emirates (1999) and Carlton & United Breweries (2000–2001).

- match records
- Team

1. Australia is the most successful Test team in cricketing history. It has won more than 350 Test matches at a rate of almost 47%. The next best performance is by South Africa at 37%.
2. Australia have been involved in the only two Tied Tests played. The first occurred in December 1960, against the West Indies in Brisbane.The second occurred in September 1986, against India in Madras (Chennai).
3. Australia's largest victory in a Test match came on 24 February 2002. Australia defeated South Africa by an innings and 360 runs in Johannesburg.
4. Australia holds the record for the most consecutive wins with 16. This has been achieved twice; from October 1999 to February 2001 and from December 2005 to January 2008.
5. Australia shares the record for the most consecutive series victories winning 9 series from October 2005 to June 2008. This record is shared with England.
6. Australia's highest total in a Test match innings was recorded in Kingston, Jamaica against the West Indies in June 1955. Australia posted 758/8 in their first innings, with five players scoring a century.
7. Australia's lowest total in a Test match innings was recorded in Birmingham against England in May 1902. Australia were bowled all out for 36.
8. Australia are the only team to have lost a Test match after enforcing the follow-on, having been the losing side in all three such matches
9. The first Test in the 1894–95 Ashes.
10. The third Test of the 1981 Ashes.
11. The second Test in the 2000–01 Border-Gavaskar Trophy series against India.
12. Against India in March 2013, Australia became the first team in Test history to declare in their first innings and then lose by an innings.
13. In the 2013–14 Ashes series, Australia took all 100 wickets on offer in the 5–0 sweep over England.
14. Ricky Ponting and Steve Waugh have played in the most Test matches for Australia, both playing in 168 matches.

- Batting

1. Charles Bannerman faced the first ball in Test cricket, scored the first runs in Test cricket and also scored the first Test century.
2. Charles Bannerman also scored 67.34% of the Australian first innings total in match 1. This record remains to this day as the highest percentage of a completed innings total that has been scored by a single batsman.
3. Ricky Ponting has scored the most runs for Australia in Test cricket with 13,378 runs. Allan Border is second with 11,174 runs in 265 innings a record which was broken by Brian Lara during his innings of 226 against Australia while Steve Waugh has 10,927 in 260 innings.Allan Border was the first Australian batsman to pass 10,000 and the first ever batsman to pass 11,000 Test runs.Ricky Ponting was the first Australian batsman to pass 12,000 and 13,000 Test runs.
4. Matthew Hayden holds the record for the most runs in a single innings by an Australian with 380 in the first Test against Zimbabwe in Perth in October 2003.
5. Donald Bradman holds the record for the highest average by an Australian (or any other) cricketer of 99.94 runs per dismissal. Bradman played 52 Tests, scoring 29 centuries and a further 13 fifties.
6. Ricky Ponting holds the record for the most centuries by an Australian cricketer with 41. Former Australian captain Steve Waugh is in second position with 32 centuries from 260 innings.
7. Allan Border holds the record for the most fifties by an Australian cricketer with 63 in 265 innings.
8. Adam Gilchrist holds the record for the fastest century by an Australian.
9. Glenn McGrath holds the record for the most ducks by an Australian cricketer with 35 in 138 innings.

- Bowling

1. Billy Midwinter picked up the first five-wicket haul in a Test innings in match 1.
2. Fred Spofforth performed Test cricket's first hat-trick by dismissing Vernon Royle, Francis McKinnon and Tom Emmett in successive balls.
3. Fred Spofforth also took the first 10-wicket match haul in Test cricket.

4. Shane Warne holds the record for the most wickets by an Australian cricketer with 708 wickets in 145 Test matches.
5. Arthur Mailey holds the record for the best bowling figures in an innings by an Australian cricketer with 9/121 against England in February 1921.
6. Bob Massie holds the record for the best bowling figures in a match by an Australian cricketer with 16/137 against England in June 1972. That was also his first Test match for Australia.
7. J. J. Ferris holds the record for the best bowling average by an Australian bowler, taking 61 wickets at 12.70 in his career.
8. Clarrie Grimmett holds the record for the most wickets in a Test series with 44 against South Africa in 1935–36.

- Fielding and wicketkeeping

1. Ricky Ponting holds the record for the most catches in a career by an Australian fielder with 196 in 168 matches.
2. Jack Blackham performed the first stumping in Test cricket in match 1.
3. Adam Gilchrist holds the record for the most dismissals in a career by an Australian wicketkeeper with 416 in 96 matches.

- Team

1. Australia's highest total in a One-Day International innings is 434/4, scored off 50 overs against South Africa in Johannesburg on 12 March 2006. This was a world record score before the South Africans later surpassed it in the same match.
2. Australia's lowest total in a One-Day International innings is 70. This score has occurred twice; once against England in 1977 and once against New Zealand in 1986.
3. Australia's largest victory in One-Day International cricket is 275 runs. This occurred against Afghanistan at the 2015 World Cup in Australia.
4. Australia are the only team in the history of the World Cup to win 3 consecutive tournaments; 1999, 2003 and 2007.
5. Australia went undefeated at the World Cup for a record 34 consecutive matches. After being defeated by Pakistan in 1999, Australia would remain unbeaten until they were again defeated by Pakistan in 2011.
6. Australia have won the most World Cups – 5.

CHAPTER FOUR

History of cricket

- History of cricket

The sport of cricket has a known history beginning in the late 16th century. Having originated in south-east England, it became an established sport in the country in the 18th century and developed globally in the 19th and 20th centuries. International matches have been played since the 19th-century and formal Test cricket matches are considered to date from 1877. Cricket is the world's second most popular spectator sport after association football (soccer).

Internationally, cricket is governed by the International Cricket Council (ICC) which has over one hundred countries and territories in membership although only twelve currently play Test cricket.

- Origin

Cricket was probably created during Saxon or Norman times by children living in the Weald, an area of dense woodlands and clearings in south-east England that lies across Kent and Sussex. The first definite written reference is from the end of the 16th-century.

There have been several speculations about the game's origins, including some that it was created in France or Flanders. The earliest of these speculative references is from 1300 and concerns the future King Edward II playing at "creag and other games" in both Westminster and Newenden. It has been suggested that "creag" was an Old English word for cricket, but expert opinion is that it was an early spelling of "craic", meaning "fun and games in general".

It is generally believed that cricket survived as a children's game for many generations before it was increasingly taken up by adults around the beginning of the 17th century. Possibly cricket was derived from bowls, assuming bowls is the older sport, by the intervention of a batsman trying to stop the ball from reaching its target by hitting it away. Playing on sheep-grazed land or in clearings, the original implements may have been a matted lump of sheep's wool (or even a stone or a small lump of wood) as the ball; a stick or a crook or another farm tool as the bat; and a stool or a tree stump or a gate (e.g., a wicket gate) as the wicket.

- First definite reference

John Derrick was a pupil at the Royal Grammar School, then the Free School, in Guildford when he and his friends played creckett circa 1550

In 1597 (Old Style – 1598 New Style) a court case in England concerning an ownership dispute over a plot of common land in Guildford, Surrey, mentions the game of creckett. A 59-year-old coroner, John Derrick, testified that he and his school friends had played creckett on the site fifty years earlier when they attended the Free School. Derrick's account proves beyond reasonable doubt that the game was being played in Surrey circa 1550, and is the earliest universally accepted reference to the game.

The first reference to cricket being played as an adult sport was in 1611, when two men in Sussex were prosecuted for playing cricket on Sunday instead of going to church. In the same year, a dictionary defined cricket as a boys‘ game, and this suggests that adult participation was a recent development.

- Derivation of the name of "cricket"

A number of words are thought to be possible sources for the term "cricket". In the earliest definite reference, it was spelled creckett. The name may have been derived from the Middle Dutch krick(-e), meaning a stick; or the Old English cricc or cryce meaning a crutch or staff, or the French word criquet meaning a wooden post. The Middle Dutch word krickstoel means a long low stool used for kneeling in church; this resembled the long low wicket with two stumps used in early cricket. According to Heiner Gillmeister, a European language expert of the University of Bonn, "cricket" derives from the Middle Dutch phrase for hockey, met de (krik ket)sen (i.e., "with the stick chase").

It is more likely that the terminology of cricket was based on words in use in south-east England at the time and, given trade connections with the County of Flanders, especially in the 15th century when it belonged to the Duchy of Burgundy, many Middle Dutch words found their way into southern English dialects.

- The Commonwealth

After the Civil War ended in 1648, the new Puritan government clamped down on "unlawful assemblies", in particular the more raucous sports such as football. Their laws also demanded a stricter observance of the Sabbath than there had been previously. As the Sabbath was the only free time available to the lower classes, cricket's popularity may have waned during the Commonwealth. However, it did flourish in public fee-paying schools such as Winchester and St Paul's. There is no actual evidence that Oliver Cromwell's regime banned cricket specifically and there are references to it during the interregnum that suggest it was acceptable to the authorities provided that it did not cause any "breach of the Sabbath". It is believed that the nobility in general adopted cricket at this time through involvement in village games.

- Gambling and press coverage

Cricket thrived after the Restoration in 1660 and is believed to have first attracted gamblers making large bets at this time. It is possible, as believed by some historians, that top-class matches began. In 1664, the "Cavalier" Parliament passed the Gaming Act 1664 which limited stakes to £100, although that was still a fortune at the time, equivalent to about £16,000 in present-day terms. Cricket had become a significant gambling sport by the end of the 17th century, as evidenced in 1697 by a newspaper report of a "great match" played in Sussex which was 11-a-side and played for high stakes of 50 guineas a side.

With freedom of the press having been granted in 1696, cricket for the first time could be reported in the newspapers. But it was a long time before the newspaper industry adapted sufficiently to provide frequent, let alone comprehensive, coverage of the game. During the first half of the 18th century, press reports tended to focus on the betting rather than on the play.

- 18th-century cricket

Gambling introduced the first patrons because some of the gamblers decided to strengthen their bets by forming their own teams and it is believed the first "county teams" were formed in the aftermath of the Restoration in 1660, especially as members of the nobility were employing "local experts" from village cricket as the earliest professionals. The first known game in which the teams use county names is in 1709 but there can be little doubt that these sort of fixtures were being arranged long before that. The match in 1697 was probably Sussex versus another county.

The most notable of the early patrons were a group of aristocrats and businessmen who were active from about 1725, which is the time that press coverage became more regular, perhaps as a result of the patrons' influence. These men included the 2nd Duke of Richmond, Sir William Gage, Alan Brodrick and Edwin Stead. For the first time, the press mentions individual players like Thomas Waymark.

- Cricket expands beyond England

Cricket was introduced to North America via the English colonies in the 17th century, probably before it had even reached the north of England. In the 18th century it arrived in other parts of the globe. It was introduced to the West Indies by colonists and to India by East India Company mariners in the first half of the century. It arrived in Australia almost as soon as colonisation began in 1788. New Zealand and South Africa followed in the early years of the 19th century.

Cricket never caught on in Canada, despite efforts by the upper class to promote the game as a way of identifying with the "mother country". Canada, unlike Australia and the West Indies, witnessed a continual decline in the popularity of the game during 1860 to 1960. Linked in the public consciousness to an upper-class sport, the game never became popular with the general public. In the summer season it had to compete with baseball. During the First World War, Canadian units stationed in France played baseball instead of cricket.

- Development Laws of Cricket

It's not clear when the basic rules of cricket such as bat and ball, the wicket, pitch dimensions, overs, how out, etc. were originally formulated. In 1728, the Duke of Richmond and Alan Brodick drew up Articles of Agreement to determine the code of practice in a particular game and this became a common feature, especially around payment of stake money and distributing the winnings given the importance of gambling.

In 1744, the Laws of Cricket were codified for the first time and then amended in 1774, when innovations such as lbw, middle stump and maximum bat width were added. These laws stated that "the principals shall choose from amongst the gentlemen present two umpires who shall absolutely decide all disputes". The codes were drawn up by the so-called "Star and Garter Club" whose members ultimately founded the Marylebone Cricket Club at Lord's in 1787. The MCC immediately became the custodian of the Laws and has made periodic revisions and recodifications subsequently.

- Continued growth in England

The game continued to spread throughout England, and, in 1751, Yorkshire is first mentioned as a venue. The original form of bowling (i.e., rolling the ball along the ground as in bowls) was superseded sometime after 1760 when bowlers began to pitch the ball and study variations in line, length and pace. Scorecards began to be kept on a regular basis from 1772; since then, an increasingly clear picture has emerged of the sport's development.

- An artwork depicting the history of the cricket bat

The first famous clubs were London and Dartford in the early 18th century. London played its matches on the Artillery Ground, which still exists. Others followed, particularly Slindon in Sussex, which was backed by the Duke of Richmond and featured the star player Richard Newland. There were other prominent clubs at Maidenhead, Hornchurch, Maidstone, Sevenoaks, Bromley, Addington, Hadlow and Chertsey.

But far and away the most famous of the early clubs was Hambledon in Hampshire. It started as a parish organisation that first achieved prominence in 1756. The club itself was founded in the 1760s and was well patronised to the extent that it was the focal point of the game for about thirty years until the formation of MCC and the opening of Lord's Cricket Ground in 1787. Hambledon produced several outstanding players including the master batsman John Small and the first great fast bowler Thomas Brett. Their most notable opponent was the Chertsey and Surrey bowler Edward "Lumpy" Stevens, who is believed to have been the main proponent of the flighted delivery.

It was in answer to the flighted, or pitched, delivery that the straight bat was introduced. The old "hockey stick"–style of bat was only really effective against the ball being trundled or skimmed along the ground. First-class cricket began, retrospectively, in 1772.A Game of Cricket at The Royal Academy Club in Marylebone Fields, now Regent's Park, depiction by unknown artist, c. 1790–1799

- History of cricket (1772–1815) and History of English cricket (1816–1863)

The game also underwent a fundamental change of organisation with the formation for the first time of county clubs. All the modern county clubs, starting with Sussex in 1839, were founded during the 19th century. No sooner had the first county clubs established themselves than they faced what amounted to "player action" as William Clarke created the travelling All-England Eleven in 1846. Though a commercial venture, this team did much to popularise the game in districts which had never previously been visited by high-class cricketers. Other similar teams were created and this vogue lasted for about thirty years. But the counties and MCC prevailed.

- A cricket match at Darnall, Sheffield in the 1820s.

The growth of cricket in the mid and late 19th century was assisted by the development of the railway network. For the first time, teams from a long distance apart could play one other without a prohibitively time-consuming journey. Spectators could travel longer distances to matches, increasing the size of crowds. Army units around the Empire had time on their hands, and encouraged the locals so they could have some entertaining competition. Most of the Empire embraced cricket, with the exception of Canada.

In 1864, another bowling revolution resulted in the legalisation of overarm and in the same year. W. G. Grace began his long and influential career at this time, his feats doing much to increase cricket's popularity.

He introduced technical innovations which revolutionised the game, particularly in batting.

- International cricket begins

The first ever international cricket game was between the US and Canada in 1844. The match was played at the grounds of the St George's Cricket Club in New York.

- The English team 1859 on their way to the US

In 1859, a team of leading English professionals set off to North America on the first-ever overseas tour and, in 1862, the first English team toured Australia. Between May and October 1868, a team of Aboriginal Australians toured England in what was the first Australian cricket team to travel overseas.

- The first Australian touring team (1878) pictured at Niagara Falls

In 1877, an England touring team in Australia played two matches against full Australian XIs that are now regarded as the inaugural Test matches. The following year, the Australians toured England for the first time and the success of this tour ensured a popular demand for similar ventures in future. No Tests were played in 1878 but more soon followed and, at The Oval in 1882, the Australian victory in a tense finish gave rise to The Ashes.South Africa became the third Test nation in 1889.

- National championships

A significant development in domestic cricket occurred in 1890 when the official County Championship was constituted in England. Soon afterwards, in May 1894, the sport's first-class standard was officially defined. This organisational initiativc has been repeated in other countries. Australia established the Sheffield Shield in 1892–93. Other national competitions to be established were the Currie Cup in South Africa, the Plunket Shield in New Zealand and the Ranji Trophy in India. The ICC re-defined first-class status in 1947 as a global concept.

The period from 1890 to the outbreak of the First World War has become one of nostalgia, ostensibly because the teams played cricket according to "the spirit of the game", but more realistically because it was a peacetime period that was shattered by the First World War. The era has been called The Golden Age of cricket and it featured numerous great names such as Grace, Wilfred Rhodes, C. B. Fry, Ranjitsinhji and Victor Trumper.

- Balls per over

During most of the 19th-century standard overs were made up of four deliveries. In 1889 five-ball overs were introduced in first-class cricket, with a move to generally use six-ball overs in 1900.

In the 20th-century, eight-ball overs were used at times in a number of countries, primarily Australia, where eight-balls were the standard over length between 1918/19 and 1978/79, South Africa and New Zealand. Since the 1979/80 Australian and New Zealand seasons, six balls per over have been used worldwide, and the most recent version of the Laws only permits six-ball overs.

- Growth of international cricket

Sid Barnes traps Lala Amarnath lbw in the first official Test between Australia and India at the MCG in 1948

The Imperial Cricket Conference was founded in 1909 with England, Australia and South Africa as the founder members. This aimed to regulate international cricket between the three sides, considered the only three of equal status at the time. West Indies were admitted as members in 1928, allowing them to play Test cricket against the other sides. New Zealand and India both became Test playing nations before World War II and Pakistan joined soon afterwards in 1952.

At the initial suggestion of Pakistan, the ICC was expanded to include non-Test playing countries from 1965, with Associate members being admitted. At the same time the organisation changed its name to the International Cricket Conference. The first limited-overs World Cups were played during the 1970s and Sri Lanka became the first Associate member to be raised to Test playing status in 1982.

The international game continued to grow with the introduction of Affiliate Member status in 1984, a level of membership designed for sides with less history of playing cricket. In 1989 the ICC renamed itself the International Cricket Council. Zimbabwe became Full Members in 1992 and Bangladesh in 2000 before Afghanistan and Ireland were both admitted as Test sides in 2018, bringing the number of full members of the ICC to 12.

- International cricket in South Africa from 1971 to 1981

The greatest crisis to hit international cricket was brought about by apartheid, the South African policy of racial segregation. The situation began to crystallise after 1961 when South Africa left the Commonwealth of Nations and so, under the rules of the day, its cricket board had to leave the International Cricket Conference (ICC). Cricket's opposition to apartheid intensified in 1968 with the cancellation of England's tour to South Africa by the South African authorities, due to the inclusion in the England team of Basil D'Oliveira, a Cape Coloured player. In 1970, the ICC members voted to suspend South Africa indefinitely from international cricket competition.

Starved of top-level competition for its best players, the South African Cricket Board began funding so-called "rebel tours", offering large sums of money for international players to form teams and tour South Africa. The ICC's response was to blacklist any rebel players who agreed to tour South Africa, banning them from officially sanctioned international cricket. As players were poorly remunerated during the 1970s, several accepted the offer to tour South Africa, particularly players getting towards the end of their careers for which a blacklisting would have little effect.

The rebel tours continued into the 1980s but then progress was made in South African politics and it became clear that apartheid was ending. South Africa, now a "Rainbow Nation" under Nelson Mandela, was welcomed back into international sport in 1991.

- World Series Cricket

The money problems of top cricketers were also the root cause of another cricketing crisis that arose in 1977 when the Australian media magnate Kerry Packer fell out with the Australian Cricket Board over TV rights. Taking advantage of the low remuneration paid to players, Packer retaliated by signing several of the best players in the world to a privately run cricket league outside the structure of international cricket. World Series Cricket hired some of the banned South African players and allowed them to show off their skills in an international arena against other world-class players. The schism lasted only until 1979 and the "rebel" players were allowed back into established international cricket, though many found that their national teams had moved on without them. Long-term results of World Series Cricket have included the introduction of significantly higher player salaries and innovations such as coloured kit and night games.

- Limited-overs cricket

In the 1960s, English county teams began playing a version of cricket with games of only one innings each and a maximum number of overs per innings. Starting in 1963 as a knockout competition only, limited-overs cricket grew in popularity and, in 1969, a national league was created which consequently caused a reduction in the number of matches in the County Championship. The status of limited overs matches is governed by the official List A categorisation. Although many "traditional" cricket fans objected to the shorter form of the game, limited-overs cricket did have the advantage of delivering a result to spectators within a single day; it did improve cricket's appeal to younger or busier people; and it did prove commercially successful.

The first limited-overs international match took place at Melbourne Cricket Ground in 1971 as a time-filler after a Test match had been abandoned because of heavy rain on the opening days. It was tried simply as an experiment and to give the players some exercise, but turned out to be immensely popular. limited-overs internationals (LOIs or ODIs—one-day internationals) have since grown to become a massively popular form of the game, especially for busy people who want to be able to see a whole match. The International Cricket Council reacted to this development by organising the first Cricket World Cup in England in 1975, with all the Test-playing nations taking part.

- Analytic and graphic technology

Limited-overs cricket increased television ratings for cricket coverage. Innovative techniques introduced in coverage of limited-over matches were soon adopted for Test coverage. The innovations included presentation of in-depth statistics and graphical analysis, placing miniature cameras in the stumps, multiple usage of cameras to provide shots from several locations around the ground, high-speed photography and computer graphics technology enabling television viewers to study the course of a delivery and help them understand an umpire's decision.

In 1992, the use of a third umpire to adjudicate run-out appeals with television replays was introduced in the Test series between South Africa and India. The third umpire's duties have subsequently expanded to include decisions on other aspects of play such as stumpings, catches and boundaries. From 2011, the third umpire was being called upon to moderate review of umpires' decisions, including lbw, with the aid of virtual-reality tracking technologies (e.g., Hawk-Eye and Hot Spot), though such measures still could not free some disputed decisions from heated controversy.

- 21st-century cricket

In June 2001, the ICC introduced a "Test Championship Table" and, in October 2002, a "One-day International Championship Table". As indicated by ICC rankings, the various cricket formats have continued to be a major competitive sport in most former British Empire countries, notably the Indian subcontinent, and new participants including the Netherlands. In 2017, the number of countries with full ICC membership was increased to twelve by the addition of Afghanistan and Ireland.

The ICC expanded its development programme, aiming to produce more national teams capable of competing at the various formats. Development efforts are focused on African and Asian nations, and on the United States. In 2004, the ICC Intercontinental Cup brought first-class cricket to 12 nations, mostly for the first time. Cricket's newest innovation is Twenty20, essentially an evening entertainment. It has so far enjoyed enormous popularity and has attracted large attendances at matches as well as good TV audience ratings. The inaugural ICC Twenty20 World Cup tournament was held in 2007. The formation of Twenty20 leagues in India – the unofficial Indian Cricket League, which started in 2007, and the official Indian Premier League, starting in 2008 – raised much speculation in the cricketing press about their effect on the future of cricket.

9 798885 556675

Printed by Libri Plureos GmbH in Hamburg, Germany